Promises for New Believers

Presented to _____

Give[n] by _____

Date _____

These are written so that you
may believe Jesus is the Messiah.
John 20:31

Bible Promises for New Believers

B&H
PUBLISHING GROUP

Nashville, Tennessee

Contents

Promises That Go Way Back

Welcome into a community of believers that stretches around the world and many centuries into the distant past. This is truly a great big family you're in, and God has blessed you—and us—by making you a part of it.

But really, this experience we call *salvation* reaches even farther back than the history of the world . . . where God has always existed, always loved you, and always been exactly who He is.

Use the next few pages to learn a little about the God you now serve. From His own words.

The Basics of Salvation

Tell Me Again What All of This Means

God loved the world in this way: He gave His One and Only Son, so that everyone who believes in Him will not perish but have eternal life. For God did not send His Son into the world that He might judge the world, but that the world might be saved through Him.

John 3:16-17

Love consists in this: not that we loved God, but that He loved us and sent His Son to be the propitiation for our sins.

1 John 4:10

This saying is trustworthy and deserving of full acceptance: "Christ Jesus came into the world to save sinners"—and I am the worst of them. But I received mercy because of this, so that in me, the worst of them, Christ Jesus might demonstrate the utmost patience.

1 Timothy 1:15-16

Whoever confesses that Jesus is the Son of God—God remains in him and he in God.

1 John 4:15

There is salvation in no one else, for there is no other name under heaven given to people by which we must be saved.

Acts 4:12

How will we escape if we neglect such a great salvation?

Hebrews 2:3

**We wouldn't have required such love
if it weren't for a big problem we had.**
*The moment we came into the world, we were
already sinful and in need of a Savior. For us to
approach a holy God, He had to change us first.*

The LORD's hand is not too short to save,
and His ear is not too deaf to hear. But your
iniquities have built barriers between you and
your God, and your sins have made Him hide
His face from you so that He does not listen.

Isaiah 59:1-2

Your guilty acts have diverted these things
from you. Your sins have withheld the bounty
from you.

Jeremiah 5:25

By nature we were children under wrath, as
the others were also. But God, who is abundant in mercy, because of His great love that
He had for us, made us alive with the Messiah
even though we were dead in trespasses.

Ephesians 2:3-5

While we were still helpless, at the appointed moment, Christ died for the ungodly.

For rarely will someone die for a just person —though for a good person perhaps someone might even dare to die. But God proves His own love for us in that while we were still sinners Christ died for us! . . .

For if, while we were enemies, we were reconciled to God through the death of His Son, then how much more, having been reconciled, will we be saved by His life!

Romans 5:6-8, 10

Therefore, since we have been declared righteous by faith, we have peace with God through our Lord Jesus Christ.

Romans 5:1

This is the message of faith that we proclaim: if you confess with your mouth, "Jesus is Lord," and believe in your heart that God raised Him from the dead, you will be saved.

With the heart one believes, resulting in righteousness, and with the mouth one confesses, resulting in salvation.

Now the Scripture says, "No one who believes on Him will be put to shame," for there is no distinction between Jew and Greek, since the same Lord of all is rich to all who call on Him. For "everyone who calls on the name of the Lord will be saved."

Romans 10:8-13

So your sin has been dealt with, your spirit reborn, your hope made secure. *God's gift of salvation has changed you into an entirely new creation—a person who no longer needs to fear the past, the present, or the future.*

What then are we to say about these things? If God is for us, who is against us? He did not even spare His own Son, but offered Him up for us all; how will He not also with Him grant us everything?

Romans 8:31-32

For by grace you are saved through faith, and this is not from yourselves; it is God's gift—not from works, so that no one can boast.

Ephesians 2:8-9

But to all who did receive Him, He gave them the right to be children of God, to those who believe in His name, who were born, not of blood, or of the will of the flesh, or of the will of man, but of God.

John 1:12-13

The Fatherhood of God

Is He to Be Feared, to Be Loved, or Both?

Look at how great a love the Father has given us, that we should be called God's children. And we are! The reason the world does not know us is that it didn't know Him.

Dear friends, we are God's children now, and what we will be has not yet been revealed. We know that when He appears, we will be like Him, because we will see Him as He is.

1 John 3:1-2

You, LORD, are our Father; from ancient times, Your name is our Redeemer.

Isaiah 63:16

And if you address as Father the One who judges impartially based on each one's work, you are to conduct yourselves in reverence during this time of temporary residence.

1 Peter 1:17

For this reason I bow my knees before the Father from whom every family in heaven and on earth is named.

Ephesians 3:14-15

For us there is one God, the Father, from whom are all things, and we for Him.

1 Corinthians 8:6

We are the clay, and You are our potter.

Isaiah 64:8

Be perfect, therefore, as your heavenly Father is perfect.

Matthew 5:48

God is fully deserving of our awe and respect. Yet He's also our loving Father.

Just as His righteous authority motivates us to obedience, His merciful heart beckons us close. We love and honor Him . . . all at the same time.

As a father has compassion on his children, so the LORD has compassion on those who fear Him.

Psalm 103:13

Look at the birds: they don't sow or reap or gather into barns, yet your heavenly Father feeds them. Aren't you worth more than they?

Matthew 6:26

What man among you, if his son asks him for bread, will give him a stone? Or if he asks for a fish, will give him a snake? If you then, who are evil, know how to give good gifts to your children, how much more will your Father in heaven give good things to those who ask!

Matthew 7:9-11

What do you think? If a man has 100 sheep, and one of them goes astray, won't he leave the 99 on the hillside, and go and search for the stray? And if he finds it, I assure you: He rejoices over that sheep more than over the 99 that did not go astray. In the same way, it is not the will of your Father in heaven that one of these little ones perish.

Matthew 18:12-14

Don't be afraid, little flock, because your Father delights to give you the kingdom.

Luke 12:32

I will be a Father to you, and you will be sons and daughters to Me, says the Lord Almighty.

2 Corinthians 6:18

Do not take the Lord's discipline lightly, or faint when you are reproved by Him; for the Lord disciplines the one He loves, and punishes every son whom He receives.

Endure it as discipline: God is dealing with you as sons. For what son is there whom a father does not discipline? But if you are without discipline—which all receive—then you are illegitimate children and not sons.

Furthermore, we had natural fathers discipline us, and we respected them. Shouldn't we submit even more to the Father of spirits and live? For they disciplined us for a short time based on what seemed good to them, but He does it for our benefit, so that we can share His holiness.

Hebrews 12:5-10

The Father knows you better than anyone, and still chooses to love you.

It is only because of His grace and mercy that we are able to receive salvation. Rest in the love He has for you—a love He'll have for you forever.

Every generous act and every perfect gift is from above, coming down from the Father of lights; with Him there is no variation or shadow cast by turning.

James 1:17

May you be strengthened with all power, according to His glorious might, for all endurance and patience, with joy giving thanks to the Father, who has enabled you to share in the saints' inheritance in the light.

He has rescued us from the domain of darkness and transferred us into the kingdom of the Son He loves, in whom we have redemption, the forgiveness of sins.

Colossians 1:11-14

The Love of Jesus Christ

Why Would He Do So Much for Me?

I am the good shepherd. The good shepherd lays down his life for the sheep.

The hired man, since he's not the shepherd and doesn't own the sheep, leaves them and runs away when he sees a wolf coming . . . because he is a hired man and doesn't care about the sheep. I am the good shepherd. I know My own sheep, and they know Me.

John 10:11-14

Long ago God spoke to the fathers by the prophets at different times and in different ways. In these last days, He has spoken to us by His Son, whom He has appointed heir of all things and through whom He made the universe. He is the radiance of His glory, the exact expression of His nature, and He sustains all things by His powerful word.

Hebrews 1:1-3

All the prophets testify about Him that through His name everyone who believes in Him will receive forgiveness of sins.

Acts 10:43

He Himself bore our sins in His body on the tree, so that, having died to sins, we might live for righteousness. . . . For you were like sheep going astray, but you have now returned to the shepherd and guardian of your souls.

1 Peter 2:24-25

For the Son of Man has come to seek and to save the lost.

Luke 19:10

Jesus endured it all for us—the pain of death, the stab of rejection—all of it. *But He did it because He loved us. He did it to guarantee us a place at the table in His heavenly kingdom. Have you ever known love like that?*

He was in the world, and the world was created through Him, yet the world did not know Him. He came to His own, and His own people did not receive Him.

John 1:10-11

He was despised and rejected by men, a man of suffering who knew what sickness was. He was someone people turned away from; He was despised, and we didn't value Him. Yet our sicknesses He himself bore, and our pains He carried.

But we in turn regarded Him to be stricken, struck down by God, and afflicted. . . . Yet He did not open His mouth. Like a lamb led to the slaughter and like a sheep silent before her shearers, He did not open His mouth.

Isaiah 53:3-4, 7

But He was pierced because of our transgressions, crushed because of our iniquities; punishment came to Him bringing us peace, and we are healed by His wounds.

Isaiah 53:5

I have been crucified with Christ; and I no longer live, but Christ lives in me. The life I now live in the flesh, I live by faith in the Son of God, who loved me and gave Himself for me.

Galatians 2:19-20

Walk in love, as the Messiah also loved us and gave Himself for us, a sacrificial and fragrant offering to God.

Ephesians 5:2

Who can separate us from the love of Christ? Can affliction or anguish or persecution or famine or nakedness or danger or sword? As it is written: "Because of You we are being put to death all day long; we are counted as sheep to be slaughtered."

No, in all these things we are more than victorious through Him who loved us.

For I am persuaded that neither death nor life, nor angels nor rulers, nor things present, nor things to come, nor powers, nor height, nor depth, nor any other created thing will have the power to separate us from the love of God that is in Christ Jesus our Lord!

Romans 8:35-39

Jesus is every bit God, yet He took on our humanity to save us from ourselves. *Through Him, through His perfect sacrifice, we have clear access to the Father. Never take lightly what Jesus Christ has taken on Himself for us.*

God has given us eternal life, and this life is in His Son.

1 John 5:11

Make your own attitude that of Christ Jesus, who, existing in the form of God, did not consider equality with God as something to be used for His own advantage. Instead He emptied Himself by assuming the form of a slave, taking on the likeness of men. And when He had come as a man in His external form, He humbled Himself by becoming obedient to the point of death—even to death on a cross.

Philippians 2:5-8

On Him God the Father has set His seal of approval.

John 6:27

The Gift of the Holy Spirit

Help Me Understand What He Can Do

You also, when you heard the word of truth, the gospel of your salvation—in Him when you believed—were sealed with the promised Holy Spirit. He is the down payment of our inheritance, for the redemption of the possession, to the praise of His glory.

Ephesians 1:13-14

When the goodness and love for man appeared from God our Savior, He saved us —not by works of righteousness that we had done, but according to His mercy, through the washing of regeneration and renewal by the Holy Spirit. This Spirit He poured out on us abundantly through Jesus Christ our Savior, so that having been justified by His grace, we may become heirs with the hope of eternal life.

Titus 3:4-7

The Spirit Himself testifies together with our spirit that we are God's children, and if children, also heirs—heirs of God and co-heirs with Christ—seeing that we suffer with Him so that we may also be glorified with Him.

Romans 8:16-17

He is the Spirit of truth, whom the world is unable to receive because it doesn't see Him or know Him. But you do know Him, because He remains with you and will be in you.

John 14:17

The Spirit has set you free to live for God in a way you never could before.
People who live without Christ may give you the impression that they are free. But the Spirit frees us to live and experience the truth . . . every day.

Now the Lord is the Spirit; and where the Spirit of the Lord is, there is freedom.
2 Corinthians 3:17

The fruit of the Spirit is love, joy, peace, patience, kindness, goodness, faith, gentleness, self-control. Against such things there is no law.
Galatians 5:22-23

I say then, walk by the Spirit and you will not carry out the desire of the flesh. For the flesh desires what is against the Spirit, and the Spirit desires what is against the flesh; these are opposed to each other, so that you don't do what you want. But if you are led by the Spirit, you are not under the law.
Galatians 5:16-18

Now there are different gifts, but the same Spirit. . . . And there are different activities, but the same God is active in everyone and everything. A manifestation of the Spirit is given to each person to produce what is beneficial.

1 Corinthians 12:4, 6-7

Do you not know that your body is a sanctuary of the Holy Spirit who is in you, whom you have from God? You are not your own, for you were bought at a price; therefore glorify God in your body.

1 Corinthians 6:19-20

Guard, through the Holy Spirit who lives in us, that good thing entrusted to you.

2 Timothy 1:14

The mind-set of the flesh is hostile to God because it does not submit itself to God's law, for it is unable to do so. Those whose lives are in the flesh are unable to please God.

You, however, are not in the flesh, but in the Spirit, since the Spirit of God lives in you. But if anyone does not have the Spirit of Christ, he does not belong to Him.

Now if Christ is in you, the body is dead because of sin, but the Spirit is life because of righteousness. And if the Spirit of Him who raised Jesus from the dead lives in you, then He who raised Christ from the dead will also bring your mortal bodies to life through His Spirit who lives in you.

Romans 8:7-11

The Spirit is our counselor, teacher, and guide, showing us the ways of God. *Because He is one with both the Father and the Son, the Spirit who lives in us can be trusted to help us understand God better all the time.*

When the Spirit of truth comes, He will guide you into all the truth.

John 16:13

For the Spirit searches everything, even the deep things of God. For who among men knows the concerns of a man except the spirit of the man that is in him? In the same way, no one knows the concerns of God except the Spirit of God.

1 Corinthians 2:10-11

The Spirit also joins to help in our weakness, because we do not know what to pray for as we should, but the Spirit Himself intercedes for us with unspoken groanings.

Romans 8:26

Promises That Begin Every Day

You've been saved for all time, but the process of experiencing this wonder begins new every morning. Each day offers you a fresh way to understand Christ's forgiveness, to sense His love, to put real truth into real life.

So whether it's waking up to pray and read your Bible, turning off the TV at night to study, or making sure you're part of a church body that proclaims the true gospel, God has built some great opportunities into the next twenty-four hours for you to feel right at home with Him.

A Time to Be Quiet

What Does Growing in Christ Require?

Come to Me, all you who are weary and burdened, and I will give you rest. Take My yoke upon you and learn from Me, because I am gentle and humble in heart, and you will find rest for your souls. For My yoke is easy and My burden is light.

Matthew 11:28-30

It is good to praise the LORD, to sing praise to Your name, Most High, to declare Your faithful love in the morning and Your faithfulness at night.

Psalm 92:1-2

The apostles gathered around Jesus and reported to Him all that they had done and taught. He said to them, "Come away by yourselves to a remote place and rest a little."

Mark 6:30-31

Rest in God alone, my soul, for my hope comes from Him. He alone is my rock and my salvation, my stronghold; I will not be shaken. My salvation and glory depend on God; my strong rock, my refuge, is in God. Trust in Him at all times, you people; pour out your hearts before Him.

Psalm 62:5-8

Teach me, and I will be silent.

Job 6:24

**In quiet times with God, you'll hear
all you'll need for the rest of the day.**
*In prayer, in Bible study, or simply in sitting still
and listening, you'll love what God has to show
you when you're quiet enough to pay attention.*

God, Your faithful love is so valuable that
people take refuge in the shadow of Your wings.
They are filled from the abundance of Your
house; You let them drink from Your refreshing
stream, for with You is life's fountain. In Your
light we will see light.

Psalm 36:7-9

The hidden things belong to the LORD our
God, but the revealed things belong to us and
our children forever, so that we may follow all
the words of this law.

Deuteronomy 29:29

For nothing is concealed except to be revealed,
and nothing hidden except to come to light.

Mark 4:22

The one who lives under the protection of the Most High dwells in the shadow of the Almighty.

Psalm 91:1

He lets me lie down in green pastures; He leads me beside quiet waters. He renews my life.

Psalm 23:2-3

Let us then make every effort to enter that rest, so that no one will fall into the same pattern of disobedience.

Hebrews 4:11

Return to your rest, my soul, for the LORD has been good to you.

Psalm 116:7

Now we have not received the spirit of the world, but the Spirit who is from God, in order to know what has been freely given to us by God. We also speak these things, not in words taught by human wisdom, but in those taught by the Spirit, explaining spiritual things to spiritual people.

But the natural man does not welcome what comes from God's Spirit, because it is foolishness to him; he is not able to know it since it is evaluated spiritually. The spiritual person, however, can evaluate everything, yet he himself cannot be evaluated by anyone.

For who has known the Lord's mind, that he may instruct Him? But we have the mind of Christ.

1 Corinthians 2:12-16

So quiet the noise around you long enough to hear what God is saying.

Developing a mind that thinks like Christ begins with spending time with Him, letting Him teach you what He knows and show you who He is.

On the last and most important day of the festival, Jesus stood up and cried out, "If anyone is thirsty, he should come to Me and drink! The one who believes in Me, as the Scripture has said, will have streams of living water flow from deep within him."

John 7:37-38

Call to Me and I will answer you and tell you great and mysterious things you do not know.

Jeremiah 33:3

Go into your private room, shut your door, and pray to your Father who is in secret. And your Father who sees in secret will reward you.

Matthew 6:6

A Reason to Pray

Lord, We've Got a Lot to Talk About

Don't worry about anything, but in everything, through prayer and petition with thanksgiving, let your requests be made known to God. And the peace of God, which surpasses every thought, will guard your hearts and your minds in Christ Jesus.

Philippians 4:6-7

I call to You for help, Lord; in the morning my prayer meets You.

Psalm 88:13

At daybreak, Lord, You hear my voice; at daybreak I plead my case to You and watch expectantly.

Psalm 5:3

Let me experience Your faithful love in the morning, for I trust in You. Reveal to me the way I should go, because I long for You.

Psalm 143:8

When, on my bed, I think of You, I meditate on You during the night watches because You are my help; I will rejoice in the shadow of Your wings. I follow close to You; Your right hand holds on to me.

Psalm 63:6-8

Help us, O Lord, for we depend on You.

2 Chronicles 14:11

Unlike the false gods of other religions, our God hears, and our God responds.
How incredible to realize that no word we speak, no thought we think ever escapes the notice of our heavenly Father. He is always listening for us.

I cry aloud to God, aloud to God, and He will hear me.

Psalm 77:1

If I had been aware of malice in my heart, the LORD would not have listened. However, God has listened; He has paid attention to the sound of my prayer. May God be praised! He has not turned away my prayer or turned His faithful love from me.

Psalm 66:18-20

Be gracious to me, Lord, for I call to You all day long. . . . I set my hope on You. For You, LORD, are kind and ready to forgive, abundant in faithful love to all who call on You.

Psalm 86:3-5

As for me, I will watch for the LORD; I will wait for the God who saves me. My God will hear me.

Micah 7:7

For we do not have a high priest who is unable to sympathize with our weaknesses, but One who has been tested in every way as we are, yet without sin. Therefore let us approach the throne of grace with boldness, so that we may receive mercy and find grace to help us at the proper time.

Hebrews 4:15-16

Because your Father knows the things you need before you ask Him.

Matthew 6:8

You should pray like this:
  Our Father in heaven,
    Your name be honored as holy.
  Your kingdom come.
    Your will be done
    on earth as it is in heaven.
  Give us today our daily bread.
    And forgive us our debts,
    as we also have forgiven our debtors.
  And do not bring us into temptation,
    but deliver us from the evil one.
  For Yours is the kingdom and the power
    and the glory forever. Amen.

Matthew 6:9-13

So make it a habit to be in constant communication—anywhere you are.
Any place can be a place of prayer—your bedside, your driver's seat, your sink when you're washing the dishes. The conversation never has to stop.

The LORD is near all who call out to Him, all who call out to Him with integrity. He fulfills the desires of those who fear Him; He hears their cry for help and saves them.

Psalm 145:18-19

Keep asking, and it will be given to you. Keep searching, and you will find. Keep knocking, and the door will be opened to you.

Matthew 7:7

Stay awake and pray, so that you won't enter into temptation. The spirit is willing, but the flesh is weak.

Matthew 26:41

Pray constantly.

1 Thessalonians 5:17

A Hunger to Study

I Want the Bible to Come Alive for Me

Continue in what you have learned and firmly believed, knowing those from whom you learned, and that from childhood you have known the sacred Scriptures, which are able to instruct you for salvation through faith in Christ Jesus.

2 Timothy 3:14-15

All Scripture is inspired by God and is profitable for teaching, for rebuking, for correcting, for training in righteousness, so that the man of God may be complete, equipped for every good work.

2 Timothy 3:16-17

For whatever was written before was written for our instruction, so that through our endurance and through the encouragement of the Scriptures we may have hope.

Romans 15:4

Open my eyes so that I may see wonderful things in Your law.

Psalm 119:18

For the word of God is living and effective and sharper than any two-edged sword, penetrating as far as to divide soul, spirit, joints, and marrow; it is a judge of the ideas and thoughts of the heart.

Hebrews 4:12

Having a Bible is like holding the truth of the ages, right in your hand.

It's a Word that continues to speak, the voice of God's Spirit revealing who He is, the beat of God's heart, teaching you what really matters.

LORD, Your word is forever; it is firmly fixed in heaven.

Psalm 119:89

The entirety of Your word is truth, and all Your righteous judgments endure forever.

Psalm 119:160

The wise will be put to shame; they will be dismayed and snared. They have rejected the word of the LORD, so what wisdom do they really have?

Jeremiah 8:9

I have Your decrees as a heritage forever; indeed, they are the joy of my heart.

Psalm 119:111

Therefore, everyone who hears these words of Mine and acts on them will be like a sensible man who built his house on the rock. The rain fell, the rivers rose, and the winds blew and pounded that house. Yet it didn't collapse, because its foundation was on the rock.

But everyone who hears these words of Mine and doesn't act on them will be like a foolish man who built his house on the sand. The rain fell, the rivers rose, the winds blew and pounded that house, and it collapsed. And its collapse was great!

Matthew 7:24-27

Help me understand Your instruction, and I will obey it and follow it with all my heart.

Psalm 119:34

The instruction of the LORD
  is perfect, reviving the soul;
the testimony of the LORD is trustworthy,
  making the inexperienced wise.
The precepts of the LORD
  are right, making the heart glad;
the commandment of the LORD
  is radiant, making the eyes light up.
The fear of the LORD
  is pure, enduring forever;
the ordinances of the LORD
  are reliable and altogether righteous.
They are more desirable than gold—
  than an abundance of pure gold;
and sweeter than honey—
  than honey dripping from the comb.

Psalm 19:7-10

Find someone who can help you dig into the Bible without losing your way.
It's a big book. It can be confusing in spots. But the more you read, the more you'll understand. The more you seek, the more you'll find.

Your word is a lamp for my feet and a light on my path.

Psalm 119:105

Your instruction resides within me.

Psalm 40:8

I have treasured Your word in my heart so that I may not sin against You.

Psalm 119:11

I rejoice in the way revealed by Your decrees as much as in all riches.

Psalm 119:14

I am resolved to obey Your statutes to the very end.

Psalm 119:112

A Desire to Worship

Do You Know How Much I Love You?

Happy are the people who know the joyful shout; LORD, they walk in the light of Your presence. They rejoice in Your name all day long, and they are exalted by Your righteousness. For You are their magnificent strength.

Psalm 89:15-17

Let the redeemed of the LORD proclaim that
He has redeemed them from the hand of the foe.

Psalm 107:2

Better a day in Your courts than a thousand
anywhere else. I would rather be at the door
of the house of my God than to live in the
tents of the wicked.

Psalm 84:10

Whom do I have in heaven but You? And I
desire nothing on earth but You. My flesh and
my heart may fail, but God is the strength of
my heart, my portion forever.

Psalm 73:25-26

LORD, You are my portion and my cup of
blessing; You hold my future. The boundary
lines have fallen for me in pleasant places;
indeed, I have a beautiful inheritance.

Psalm 16:5-6

My praise is always about You.

Psalm 71:6

Nor sure what to be praising Him for? Just thank Him for what He has done.

You won't have to look far to see the thousands of things God has done in your life. Once you get started, in fact, you won't know where to stop.

Sing to the LORD, for He has done glorious things. Let this be known throughout the earth.

Isaiah 12:5

My mouth will tell about Your righteousness and Your salvation all day long, though I cannot sum them up.

Psalm 71:15

One generation will declare Your works to the next and will proclaim Your mighty acts.

Psalm 145:4

All You have made will praise You, LORD. . . . They will speak of the glory of Your kingdom and will declare Your might.

Psalm 145:10-11

Oh, the depth of the riches both of the wisdom and the knowledge of God! How unsearchable His judgments and untraceable His ways! For who has known the mind of the Lord? Or who has been His counselor? Or who has ever first given to Him, and has to be repaid? For from Him and through Him and to Him are all things.

Romans 11:33-36

Therefore, through Him let us continually offer up to God a sacrifice of praise, that is, the fruit of our lips that confess His name.

Hebrews 13:15

I will praise the LORD at all times.

Psalm 34:1

Shout triumphantly
   to the LORD, all the earth.
Serve the LORD with gladness;
   come before Him with joyful songs.
Acknowledge that the LORD is God.
   He made us, and we are His—
   His people, the sheep of His pasture.
Enter His gates with thanksgiving
   and His courts with praise.
Give thanks to Him and praise His name.
   For the LORD is good,
   and His love is eternal;
His faithfulness endures
   through all generations.

Psalm 100:1-5

You'll be praising Him forever. Why not go ahead and get good at it now?
An attitude of worship can transform the most ordinary day into a celebration of God's goodness. To see your way through life, start by looking up.

Let the message about the Messiah dwell richly among you, teaching and admonishing one another in all wisdom, and singing psalms, hymns, and spiritual songs, with gratitude in your hearts to God.

Colossians 3:16

I will sing about the LORD's faithful love forever; with my mouth I will proclaim Your faithfulness to all generations.

Psalm 89:1

You turned my lament into dancing; You removed my sackcloth and clothed me with gladness, so that I can sing to You and not be silent. LORD my God, I will praise You forever.

Psalm 30:11-12

A Church to Call Home

What Makes Sundays So Important?

Let us be concerned about one another in order to promote love and good works, not staying away from our meetings, as some habitually do, but encouraging each other, and all the more as you see the day drawing near.

Hebrews 10:24-25

How happy are those who reside in Your house, who praise You continually.

Psalm 84:4

Planted in the house of the LORD, they thrive in the courtyards of our God. They will still bear fruit in old age, healthy and green.

Psalm 92:13-14

So also you—since you are zealous in matters of the spirit, seek to excel in building up the church.

1 Corinthians 14:12

For you are all sons of God through faith in Christ Jesus. For as many of you as have been baptized into Christ have put on Christ. There is no Jew or Greek, slave or free, male or female; for you are all one in Christ Jesus.

Galatians 3:26-28

Therefore encourage one another and build each other up.

1 Thessalonians 5:11

The church is for all kinds of people who have one big thing in common.

You may not see eye-to-eye with everyone on the church roll, but God has put you all together for a reason—to glorify Him by standing united.

Now as we have many parts in one body, and all the parts do not have the same function, in the same way we who are many are one body in Christ and individually members of one another.

Romans 12:4-5

How good and pleasant it is when brothers can live together! . . . For there the LORD has appointed the blessing—life forevermore.

Psalm 133:1, 3b

The one who says he is in the light but hates his brother is in the darkness until now. The one who loves his brother remains in the light, and there is no cause for stumbling in him.

1 John 2:9-10

Now may the God of endurance and encouragement grant you agreement with one another, according to Christ Jesus, so that you may glorify the God and Father of our Lord Jesus Christ with a united mind and voice. Therefore accept one another, just as the Messiah also accepted you, to the glory of God.

Romans 15:5-7

Everyone should look out not only for his own interests, but also for the interests of others.

Philippians 2:4

Therefore, as we have opportunity, we must work for the good of all, especially for those who belong to the household of faith.

Galatians 6:10

In Christ Jesus, you who were far away have been brought near by the blood of the Messiah. . . .When Christ came, He proclaimed the good news of peace to you who were far away and peace to those who were near. For through Him we both have access by one Spirit to the Father.

So then you are no longer foreigners and strangers, but fellow citizens with the saints, and members of God's household, built on the foundation of the apostles and prophets, with Christ Jesus Himself as the cornerstone. The whole building is being fitted together in Him and is growing into a holy sanctuary in the Lord, in whom you also are being built together for God's dwelling in the Spirit.

Ephesians 2:13, 17-22

We need each other if we're to be what God wants us to be in the world.

Go out of your way to involve yourself in the church, sharing your gifts with those in need, receiving from others the gift of fellowship.

Based on the gift they have received, everyone should use it to serve others, as good managers of the varied grace of God.

1 Peter 4:10

Love must be without hypocrisy. Detest evil; cling to what is good. Show family affection to one another with brotherly love. Outdo one another in showing honor.

Romans 12:9-10

Encourage each other daily, while it is still called today, so that none of you is hardened by sin's deception.

Hebrews 3:13

Be an example to the believers.

1 Timothy 4:12

Promises That Keep You Going

Receiving Christ is easy, but living for Him—
let's face it, it's sometime a lot harder than you
might expect.

But God understands this. That's why His
Word is full of promises that belong etched in
your memory bank, underlined in your Bible,
and taped onto your bathroom mirror. These
are words of advice and encouragement from
your Father to help you realize how many of
us are going through the same exact thing—
and how big and powerful He is to help is.

When You're Tempted

I Assume Sin Isn't Going Totally Away

No temptation has overtaken you except what is common to humanity. God is faithful and He will not allow you to be tempted beyond what you are able, but with the temptation He will also provide a way of escape, so that you are able to bear it.

1 Corinthians 10:13

Dear friends, when the fiery ordeal arises among you to test you, don't be surprised by it, as if something unusual were happening to you.

1 Peter 4:12

Consider it a great joy, my brothers, whenever you experience various trials, knowing that the testing of your faith produces endurance.

James 1:2

Blessed is a man who endures trials, because when he passes the test he will receive the crown of life that He has promised to those who love Him.

James 1:12

Many adversities come to the one who is righteous, but the LORD delivers him from them all.

Psalm 34:19

The Lord knows how to rescue the godly from trials.

2 Peter 2:9

Temptation will always be a struggle, but God will always be your strength.
Sin is tricky, deceptive, misleading. So your best defense is to fill your mind so full of the truth, you'll be able to spot temptation a mile away.

There is a way that seems right to a man, but its end is the way to death.

Proverbs 14:12

For when you were slaves of sin, you were free from allegiance to righteousness. And what fruit was produced then from the things you are now ashamed of? For the end of those things is death.

Romans 6:20-21

Don't be deceived: God is not mocked. For whatever a man sows he will also reap, because the one who sows to his flesh will reap corruption from the flesh, but the one who sows to the Spirit will reap eternal life from the Spirit.

Galatians 6:7-8

No one undergoing a trial should say, "I am being tempted by God." For God is not tempted by evil, and He doesn't tempt anyone. But each person is tempted when he is drawn away and enticed by his own evil desires. Then after desire has conceived, it gives birth to sin, and when sin is fully grown, it gives birth to death.

James 1:13-15

Therefore, whoever thinks he stands must be careful not to fall!

1 Corinthians 10:12

God of our salvation, help us—for the glory of Your name. Deliver us and atone for our sins, for Your name's sake.

Psalm 79:9

He reached down from on high and took hold of me; He pulled me out of deep water. He rescued me from my powerful enemy and from those who hated me, for they were too strong for me.

They confronted me in the day of my distress, but the LORD was my support. He brought me out to a wide-open place; He rescued me because He delighted in me. . . .

He trains my hands for war; my arms can bend a bow of bronze. You have given me the shield of Your salvation; Your right hand upholds me, and Your humility exalts me. You widen a place beneath me for my steps, and my ankles do not give way.

Psalm 18:16-19, 34-36

When you see sin coming, run to get away from it, and get up close to God. *No one stands a chance against the tricks of the enemy when they're fighting alone. Flee to God, and let Him do all your fighting for you.*

Be on the alert! Your adversary the Devil is prowling around like a roaring lion, looking for anyone he can devour. Resist him, firm in the faith, knowing that the same sufferings are being experienced by your brothers in the world.

1 Peter 5:8-9

Therefore, submit to God. But resist the Devil, and he will flee from you.

James 4:7

Don't give the Devil an opportunity.

Ephesians 4:27

For the Devil has come down to you with great fury, because he knows he has a short time.

Revelation 12:12

When You've Messed Up

How Many Chances Does God Give?

Out of the depths I call to You, LORD! Lord, listen to my voice; let Your ears be attentive to my cry for help. LORD, if You considered sins, Lord, who could stand? But with You there is forgiveness, so that You may be revered.

Psalm 130:1-3

I said, "LORD, be gracious to me; heal me, for
I have sinned against You."

Psalm 41:4

If we say, "We have no sin," we are deceiving
ourselves, and the truth is not in us. If we confess our sins, He is faithful and righteous to
forgive us our sins and to cleanse us from
all unrighteousness.

1 John 1:8-9

And if My people who are called by My
name humble themselves, pray and seek My
face, and turn from their evil ways, then I will
hear from heaven, forgive their sin, and heal
their land.

2 Chronicles 7:14

You do not want a sacrifice, or I would give
it; You are not pleased with a burnt offering.
The sacrifice pleasing to God is a broken spirit.
God, You will not despise a broken and humbled heart.

Psalm 51:16-17

God doesn't hate us when we sin, but He certainly hates what sin does to us.
Failing God is only one thing that happens when we cave in to sin. We also miss out on the blessing of living in pure fellowship with the Father.

The salvation of the righteous is from the LORD, their refuge in a time of distress. The LORD helps and delivers them; He will deliver them from the wicked and will save them because they take refuge in Him.

Psalm 37:39-40

For troubles without number have surrounded me; my sins have overtaken me; I am unable to see. They are more than the hairs of my head, and my courage leaves me. LORD, be pleased to deliver me; hurry to help me, LORD.

Psalm 40:12-13

In Your presence is abundant joy; in Your right hand are eternal pleasures.

Psalm 16:11

Now if the wicked turns away from all his sins that he has done, and keeps all My statutes and practices justice and righteousness, he will surely live; he will not die. None of the transgressions that he has done will be remembered against him; because of the righteousness which he has done he will live.

Do you actually think that I take pleasure in the death of the wicked, declares the Lord GOD, and not rather that he should turn away from his ways, and live?

Ezekiel 18:21-23

Therefore, this is what the LORD says: If you return, I will restore you; you will stand in My presence.

Jeremiah 15:19

Wash away my guilt, and cleanse me from my sin. For I am conscious of my rebellion, and my sin is always before me. Against You— You alone—I have sinned and done this evil in Your sight. . . .

Purify me with hyssop, and I will be clean; wash me, and I will be whiter than snow. Let me hear joy and gladness; let the bones You have crushed rejoice. Turn Your face away from my sins and blot out all my guilt.

God, create a clean heart for me and renew a steadfast spirit within me. Do not banish me from Your presence or take Your Holy Spirit from me. Restore the joy of Your salvation to me, and give me a willing spirit.

Psalm 51:2-4, 7-12

Our sin is no surprise to God. But He loves showing us the best way out of it. *God's quickness to forgive should never be our excuse for sinning anyway. But when we've goofed up again, it's a promise we can claim real quick.*

The LORD is compassionate and gracious, slow to anger and full of faithful love. He will not always accuse us or be angry forever. He has not dealt with us as our sins deserve or repaid us according to our offenses. For as high as the heavens are above the earth, so great is His faithful love toward those who fear Him. As far as the east is from the west, so far has He removed our transgressions from us.

Psalm 103:8-12

He brought me up from a desolate pit, out of the muddy clay, and set my feet on a rock, making my steps secure. He put a new song in my mouth, a hymn of praise to our God.

Psalm 40:2-3

When You're in a Rut

What Do I Do When Life Gets Boring?

I know both how to have a little, and I know how to have a lot. In any and all circumstances I have learned the secret of being content— whether well-fed or hungry, whether in abundance or in need. I am able to do all things through Him who strengthens me.

Philippians 4:12-13

The conclusion of a matter is better than its beginning; a patient spirit is better than a proud spirit. Don't let your spirit be easily grieved, because grief possesses the heart of fools. Don't ask, "Why were the old days better than these?" For wisdom does not lead you to ask such questions.

Ecclesiastes 7:8-10

We know that all things work together for the good of those who love God: those who are called according to His purpose.

Romans 8:28

So don't throw away your confidence, which has a great reward. For you need endurance, so that after you have done God's will, you may receive what was promised.

Hebrews 10:35-36

Rejoice in hope; be patient in affliction; be persistent in prayer.

Romans 12:12

Following Christ is not an easy job. Nothing that's worthwhile ever is.

Jesus Christ is a loving Master, and we can take comfort in the fact that He loves us. But we are still in subjection to Him. We are His servants.

Which one of you having a slave plowing or tending sheep, would say to him when he comes in from the field, "Come at once and sit down to eat"? Instead, would he not tell him, "Prepare something for me to eat, get ready, and serve me while I eat and drink; later you may eat and drink.". . . In the same way, when you have done all that you were commanded, you should say, "We are good-for-nothing slaves; we've only done our duty."

Luke 17:7-10

His master said to him, "Well done, good and faithful slave! You were faithful over a few things; I will put you in charge of many things. Enter your master's joy!"

Matthew 25:21

If anyone wants to be My follower, he must deny himself, take up his cross, and follow Me. For whoever wants to save his life will lose it, but whoever loses his life because of Me and the gospel will save it.

Mark 8:34-35

So don't be ashamed of the testimony about our Lord. . . . Instead, share in suffering for the gospel, relying on the power of God, who has saved us and called us with a holy calling.

2 Timothy 1:8-9

Keep a clear head about everything, endure hardship, do the work of an evangelist, fulfill your ministry.

2 Timothy 4:5

I consider that the sufferings of this present time are not worth comparing with the glory that is going to be revealed to us. . . .

For we know that the whole creation has been groaning together with labor pains until now. And not only that, but we ourselves who have the Spirit as the firstfruits—we also groan within ourselves, eagerly waiting for adoption, the redemption of our bodies.

Now in this hope we were saved, yet hope that is seen is not hope, because who hopes for what he sees? But if we hope for what we do not see, we eagerly wait for it with patience.

Romans 8:18, 22-25

Christianity is a long-distance run . . . with one incredible pay-off at the end.

The Lord can help you find joy in the middle of a boring day, a reason to keep going, a way to give up the good in exchange for God's best.

For me, living is Christ.

Philippians 1:21

I will delight in Your statutes; I will not forget Your word. . . . Your decrees are my delight and my counselors.

Psalm 119:16, 24

Commit your way to the LORD; trust in Him, and He will act, making your righteousness shine like the dawn, your justice like the noonday.

Psalm 37:5-6

Take delight in the LORD, and He will give you your heart's desires.

Psalm 37:4

When You're Tired

Sometimes I Don't Feel Like Trying

God, hear my cry; pay attention to my prayer. I call to You from the ends of the earth when my heart is without strength. Lead me to a rock that is high above me, for You have been a refuge for me, a strong tower in the face of the enemy.

Psalm 61:1-3

Cast your burden on the LORD, and He will support you; He will never allow the righteous to be shaken.

Psalm 55:22

He gives strength to the weary, and strengthens the powerless. Youths may faint and grow weary, and young men stumble and fall, but those who trust in the LORD will renew their strength; they will soar on wings like eagles; they will run and not grow weary; they will walk and not faint.

Isaiah 40:29-31

Do not fear, for I am with you; do not be afraid, for I am your God. I will strengthen you; I will help you; I will support you with My righteous right hand.

Isaiah 41:10

So we must not get tired of doing good, for we will reap at the proper time if we don't give up.

Galatians 6:9

**It's natural to get tired along the way.
But God's strength is supernatural.**

*If you made it look easy, people would marvel at
how strong you are. But when you don't feel like
going on, they'll marvel at His strength in you.*

Although my spirit is weak within me,
You know my way.

Psalm 142:3

A man's steps are established by the LORD,
and He takes pleasure in his way.

Psalm 37:23

Therefore, I will most gladly boast all the
more about my weaknesses, so that Christ's
power may reside in me. . . . For when I am
weak, then I am strong.

2 Corinthians 12:9, 10

You will keep in perfect peace the mind that
is dependent on You, for it is trusting in You.

Isaiah 26:3

Now, this is what the LORD says—the One who created you, Jacob, and the One who formed you, Israel—"Do not fear, for I have redeemed you; I have called you by your name; you are Mine.

"I will be with you when you pass through the waters, and when you pass through the rivers, they will not overwhelm you. You will not be burned when you walk through the fire, and the flame will not burn you. For I am the LORD your God, the Holy One of Israel, your Savior."

Isaiah 43:1-3

I am guiding you on straight paths. When you walk, your steps will not be hindered; when you run, you will not stumble.

Proverbs 4:11-12

I raise my eyes toward the mountains. Where will my help come from? My help comes from the LORD, the Maker of heaven and earth. He will not allow your foot to slip; your Protector will not slumber. Indeed, the Protector of Israel does not slumber or sleep.

The LORD protects you; the LORD is a shelter right by your side. The sun will not strike you by day, or the moon by night. The LORD will protect you from all harm; He will protect your life. The LORD will protect your coming and going both now and forever.

Psalm 121:1-8

Everything you need has already been supplied. Take up your traveling gear.
God continually fills your tank with the strength and determination to fight through your feelings. Let His power overwhelm your tired excuses.

Finally, be strengthened by the Lord and by His vast strength. Put on the full armor of God so that you can stand against the tactics of the Devil. For our battle is not against flesh and blood, but against the rulers, against the authorities, against the world powers of this darkness, against the spiritual forces of evil in the heavens. This is why you must take up the full armor of God, so that you may be able to resist in the evil day, and having prepared everything, to take your stand.

Ephesians 6:10-13

If I say, "My foot is slipping," Your faithful love will support me, LORD. When I am filled with cares, Your comfort brings me joy.

Psalm 94:18-19

When You're Not So Sure

Is It Normal to Have a Few Doubts?

As He was saying these things, many believed in Him. So Jesus said to the Jews who had believed Him, "If you continue in My word, you really are My disciples. You will know the truth, and the truth will set you free."

John 8:30-32

Now faith is the reality of what is hoped for, the proof of what is not seen.

Hebrews 11:1

Faith comes from what is heard, and what is heard comes through the message about Christ.

Romans 10:17

We know that we are of God, and the whole world is under the sway of the evil one. And we know that the Son of God has come and has given us understanding so that we may know the true One. We are in the true One— that is, in His Son Jesus Christ. He is the true God and eternal life.

1 John 5:19-20

Let us draw near with a true heart in full assurance of faith, our hearts sprinkled clean from an evil conscience and our bodies washed in pure water. Let us hold on to the confession of our hope without wavering, for He who promised is faithful.

Hebrews 10:22-23

The Bible can be hard to understand. But ask God to reveal its truth to you. *He delights in opening wide the deep wells of His truth and His purposes. So get in there and start digging. Who knows what all you'll find?*

Now if any of you lacks wisdom, he should ask God, who gives to all generously and without criticizing, and it will be given to him.

James 1:5

For the time will come when they will not tolerate sound doctrine, but according to their own desires, will accumulate teachers for themselves because they have an itch to hear something new.

2 Timothy 4:3

And I pray this: that your love will keep on growing in knowledge and every kind of discernment, so that you can determine what really matters and can be pure and blameless in the day of Christ.

Philippians 1:9-10

Be doers of the word and not hearers only, deceiving yourselves. Because if anyone is a hearer of the word and not a doer, he is like a man looking at his own face in a mirror; for he looks at himself, goes away, and right away forgets what kind of man he was. But the one who looks intently into the perfect law of freedom and perseveres in it, and is not a forgetful hearer but a doer who acts—this person will be blessed in what he does.

James 1:22-25

As it is written: What no eye has seen and no ear has heard, and what has never come into a man's heart, is what God has prepared for those who love Him.

1 Corinthians 2:9

Dear friends, do not believe every spirit, but test the spirits to determine if they are from God, because many false prophets have gone out into the world.

This is how you know the Spirit of God: Every spirit who confesses that Jesus Christ has come in the flesh is from God. But every spirit who does not confess Jesus is not from God....

They are from the world. Therefore what they say is from the world, and the world listens to them. We are from God. Anyone who knows God listens to us; anyone who is not from God does not listen to us.

From this we know the Spirit of truth and the spirit of deception.

1 John 4:1-3, 5-6

Don't feel funny if you don't get it all.
None of us do. We just learn to believe.
*And on the other side of trust and belief, we find
a God who blows our mind. Would He really be
God if He wasn't bigger than our imagination?*

A man's steps are determined by the LORD,
so how can anyone understand his own way?

Proverbs 20:24

For My thoughts are not your thoughts, and
your ways are not My ways, declares the LORD.
For as heaven is higher than earth, so My ways
are higher than your ways, and My thoughts
than your thoughts.

Isaiah 55:8-9

We will no longer be little children, tossed by
the waves and blown around by every wind of
teaching, by human cunning with cleverness in
the techniques of deceit. But speaking the truth
in love, let us grow in every way into Him who
is the head—Christ.

Ephesians 4:14-15

Promises That Never End

Some people think that we've given up a lot to become believers. But what they apparently don't realize is what we've gotten in return: the true joy of giving, the blessing of belonging, the promise of forever.

Have you ever tried letting your imagination get its arms around eternity, a time when the sun never sets, the feeling never fades, and today never has to end? Try it sometime. And if you think it's just a dream, let these promises pinch you long enough to remind you that it's real.

Blessing Others

You've Been Given a Gift to Share

All of you should be like-minded and sympathetic, should love believers, and be compassionate and humble, not paying back evil for evil or insult for insult but, on the contrary, giving a blessing, since you were called for this, so that you can inherit a blessing.

1 Peter 3:8-9

Whoever wants to become great among you must be your servant, and whoever wants to be first among you must be your slave; just as the Son of Man did not come to be served, but to serve, and to give His life—a ransom for many.

Matthew 20:26-28

Everyone who exalts himself will be humbled, and the one who humbles himself will be exalted.

Luke 14:11

Give to the one who asks you, and don't turn away from the one who wants to borrow from you.

Matthew 5:42

For if you love those who love you, what reward will you have? . . . And if you greet only your brothers, what are you doing out of the ordinary?

Matthew 5:46-47

Just as you want others to do for you, do the same for them.

Luke 6:31

Giving comes with a really cool twist. It pays you back more than you give.

Some people might call it a burden to have to be constantly watching out for others' interests. They apparently don't know how much fun it can be.

If a brother or sister is without clothes and lacks daily food, and one of you says to them, "Go in peace, keep warm, and eat well," but you don't give them what the body needs, what good is it?

James 2:15-16

If anyone has this world's goods and sees his brother in need but shuts off his compassion from him—how can God's love reside in him? Little children, we must not love in word or speech, but in deed and truth.

1 John 3:17-18

Don't neglect to do good and to share, for God is pleased with such sacrifices.

Hebrews 13:16

The person who sows sparingly will also reap sparingly, and the person who sows generously will also reap generously.

Each person should do as he has decided in his heart—not out of regret or out of necessity, for God loves a cheerful giver. And God is able to make every grace overflow to you, so that in every way, always having everything you need, you may excel in every good work.

2 Corinthians 9:6-8

A generous person will be enriched.

Proverbs 11:25

May the Lord cause you to increase and over-flow with love for one another and for everyone.

1 Thessalonians 3:12

If you get rid of the yoke from those around you, the finger-pointing and malicious speaking, and if you offer yourself to the hungry, and satisfy the afflicted one, then your light will shine in the darkness, and your night will be like noonday.

The LORD will always lead you, satisfy you in a parched land, and strengthen your bones. You will be like a watered garden and like a spring whose waters never run dry.

Some of you will rebuild the ancient ruins; you will restore the foundations laid long ago; you will be called the repairer of broken walls, the restorer of streets where people live.

Isaiah 58:9-12

We've been given so much from God, we can't help but share a little around.

You'll look back on your life and be truly sorry for every day that went by without touching another's life. Start making it a point to do that today.

I have great joy and encouragement from your love, because the hearts of the saints have been refreshed through you.

Philemon 7

Keep your love for one another at full strength, since love covers a multitude of sins.

1 Peter 4:8

And be kind and compassionate to one another, forgiving one another, just as God also forgave you in Christ.

Ephesians 4:32

Carry one another's burdens; in this way you will fulfill the law of Christ.

Galatians 6:2

Sharing Jesus

What Do I Say? How Can I Explain?

Who will harm you if you are passionate for what is good? . . . Do not fear what they fear or be disturbed, but set apart the Messiah as Lord in your hearts, and always be ready to give a defense to anyone who asks you for a reason for the hope that is in you.

1 Peter 3:13-15

Who made the human mouth? Who makes him mute or deaf, seeing or blind? Is it not I, the Lord? Now go! I will help you speak and I will teach you what to say.

Exodus 4:11-12

You will receive power when the Holy Spirit has come upon you, and you will be My witnesses in Jerusalem, in all Judea and Samaria, and to the ends of the earth.

Acts 1:8

You will be brought before kings and governors because of My name. It will lead to an opportunity for you to witness. Therefore make up your minds not to prepare your defense ahead of time, for I will give you such words and a wisdom that none of your adversaries will be able to resist or contradict.

Luke 21:12-15

Tell the people all about this life.

Acts 5:20

The message isn't always easy to share, but the main idea is really very simple. *Christ has come, and Christ has died for sinners, and Christ lives today to spare us from a date with death. Just say that. See what happens.*

When I came to you, brothers, announcing the testimony of God to you, I did not come with brilliance of speech or wisdom. For I determined to know nothing among you except Jesus Christ and Him crucified. . . .

My speech and my proclamation were not with persuasive words of wisdom, but with a demonstration of the Spirit and power, so that your faith might not be based on men's wisdom but on God's power.

1 Corinthians 2:1-2, 4-5

But as for me, I will never boast about anything except the cross of our Lord Jesus Christ, through whom the world has been crucified to me, and I to the world.

Galatians 6:14

Again the next day, John was standing with two of his disciples. When he saw Jesus passing by, he said, "Look! The Lamb of God!". . . Andrew, Simon Peter's brother, was one of the two who heard John and followed Him. He first found his own brother Simon and told him, "We have found the Messiah!"

John 1:35-36, 40-41

For I am not ashamed of the gospel, because it is God's power for salvation to everyone who believes.

Romans 1:16

Because you have seen Me, you have believed. Blessed are those who believe without seeing.

John 20:29

Therefore if anyone is in Christ, there is a new creation; old things have passed away, and look, new things have come.

Now everything is from God, who reconciled us to Himself through Christ and gave us the ministry of reconciliation: that is, in Christ, God was reconciling the world to Himself, not counting their trespasses against them, and He has committed the message of reconciliation to us.

Therefore, we are ambassadors for Christ; certain that God is appealing through us, we plead on Christ's behalf, "Be reconciled to God." He made the One who did not know sin to be sin for us, so that we might become the righteousness of God in Him.

2 Corinthians 5:17-21

Be looking for someone to tell your story to. No one can argue with that. *The blessings of sharing your testimony of God's love and faithfulness are always more numerous than the excuses for staying scared and silent.*

Walk in wisdom toward outsiders, making the most of the time. Your speech should always be gracious, seasoned with salt, so that you may know how you should answer each person.

Colossians 4:5-6

For to those who are perishing the message of the cross is foolishness, but to us who are being saved it is God's power.

1 Corinthians 1:18

But I am not ashamed, because I know whom I have believed and am persuaded that He is able to guard what has been entrusted to me until that day.

2 Timothy 1:12

Seeking God

If I Could Do Just One Thing . . .

Don't worry, saying, "What will we eat?" or "What will we drink?" or "What will we wear?" For the Gentiles eagerly seek all these things, and your heavenly Father knows that you need them. But seek first the kingdom of God and His righteousness, and all these things will be provided for you.

Matthew 6:31-33

O God, You are my God; I eagerly seek You. My soul thirsts for You; my body faints for You in a land that is dry, desolate, and without water. So I gaze on You in the sanctuary to see Your strength and Your glory.

Psalm 63:1-2

Those who know Your name trust in You because You have not abandoned those who seek You, LORD.

Psalm 9:10

For I know the plans I have for you," says the LORD, "wholesome plans and not harmful, to give you a future and hope. You will call to Me and come and pray to Me. Then I will listen to you. You will seek Me and find Me if you seek for Me with all your heart."

Jeremiah 29:11-13

Let all who seek You rejoice and be glad in You; let those who love Your salvation continually say, "Great is the LORD!"

Psalm 40:16

God should always come first. How's that for keeping it pure and simple?

He loves you more than you could ever imagine, and the only things truly worth having in life are found right in the center of His will. Stay there.

Why do you spend money on what is not food, and your wages on what does not satisfy? Listen carefully to Me, and eat what is good, and you will enjoy the choicest of foods.

Isaiah 55:2

Taste and see that the LORD is good. How happy is the man who takes refuge in Him! Fear the LORD, you His saints, for those who fear Him lack nothing. Young lions lack food and go hungry, but those who seek the LORD will not lack any good thing.

Psalm 34:8-10

The humble will eat and be satisfied; those who seek the LORD will praise Him.

Psalm 22:26

Who may ascend the mountain of the LORD? Who may stand in His holy place? The one who has clean hands and a pure heart, who has not set his mind on what is false, and who has not sworn deceitfully.

He will receive blessing from the LORD, and righteousness from the God of his salvation. Such is the generation of those who seek Him, who seek the face of the God of Jacob.

Lift up your heads, O gates! Rise up, O ancient doors! Then the King of glory will come in.

Psalm 24:3-7

In Your behalf my heart says, "Seek My face." LORD, I will seek Your face.

Psalm 27:8

One of the scribes approached. When he heard them debating and saw that Jesus answered them well, he asked Him, "Which commandment is the most important of all?"

"This is the most important," Jesus answered: "'Hear, O Israel! The Lord our God is one Lord. And you shall love the Lord your God with all your heart, with all your soul, with all your mind, and with all your strength.'

"The second is: 'You shall love your neighbor as yourself.' There is no other commandment greater than these."

Mark 12:28-31

Seeking the Lord at all times gives every day a certain sense of forever.

Keep great verses like these on your short list of priorities. They'll help you remember in an instant who comes first . . . and whose way will last.

How happy are those whose way is blameless, who live according to the law of the LORD! Happy are those who keep His decrees and seek Him with all their heart.

Psalm 119:1-2

Without faith it is impossible to please God, for the one who draws near to Him must believe that He exists and rewards those who seek Him.

Hebrews 11:6

Yes, the Father wants such people to worship Him. God is Spirit, and those who worship Him must worship in spirit and truth.

John 4:23-24

For it is time to seek the LORD.

Hosea 10:12

Growing Fruit

What Is My Life Supposed to Look Like?

You did not choose Me, but I chose you.
I appointed you that you should go out and
produce fruit, and that your fruit should remain,
so that whatever you ask the Father in My name,
He will give you. This is what I command you:
that you love one another.

John 15:16-17

Therefore as you have received Christ Jesus the Lord, walk in Him, rooted and built up in Him and established in the faith, just as you were taught, and overflowing with thankfulness.

Colossians 2:6-7

Put on heartfelt compassion, kindness, humility, gentleness, and patience, accepting one another and forgiving one another if anyone has a complaint against another. Just as the Lord has forgiven you, so also you must forgive. Above all, put on love—the perfect bond of unity. And let the peace of the Messiah, to which you were also called in one body, control your hearts. Be thankful.

Colossians 3:12-15

For you were once darkness, but now you are light in the Lord. Walk as children of light—for the fruit of the light results in all goodness, righteousness, and truth—discerning what is pleasing to the Lord.

Ephesians 5:8-10

You'll never be perfect, but you can be constantly progressing, always growing. *The Spirit now lives within you, changing you from the inside out. It happens in waves, over time, as you go. But sure enough, it will happen.*

You are the light of the world. A city situated on a hill cannot be hidden. No one lights a lamp and puts it under a basket, but rather on a lampstand, and it gives light for all who are in the house. In the same way, let your light shine before men, so that they may see your good works and give glory to your Father in heaven.

Matthew 5:14-16

Therefore, whether you eat or drink, or whatever you do, do everything for God's glory.

1 Corinthians 10:31

For we are His making—created in Christ Jesus for good works, which God prepared ahead of time so that we should walk in them.

Ephesians 2:10

Do not love the world or the things that belong
to the world. If anyone loves the world, love for
the Father is not in him. Because everything that
belongs to the world—the lust of the flesh, the
lust of the eyes, and the pride in one's lifestyle—
is not from the Father, but is from the world.
And the world with its lust is passing away, but
the one who does God's will remains forever.

1 John 2:15-17

If we live by the Spirit, we must also follow
the Spirit.

Galatians 5:25

Practice these things; be committed to them,
so that your progress may be evident to all.

1 Timothy 4:15

Just as a branch is unable to produce fruit by itself unless it remains on the vine, so neither can you unless you remain in Me.

I am the vine; you are the branches. The one who remains in Me and I in him produces much fruit, because you can do nothing without Me. If anyone does not remain in Me, he is thrown aside like a branch and he withers. They gather them, throw them into the fire, and they are burned.

If you remain in Me and My words remain in you, ask whatever you want and it will be done for you. My Father is glorified by this: that you produce much fruit and prove to be My disciples.

John 15:4-8

You are now a living testimony to what Jesus can do in a person's heart.

You are being watched. People are sizing you up, wanting to see what difference it makes to be a Christian. Let them see Jesus living in you.

Therefore, brothers, by the mercies of God, I urge you to present your bodies as a living sacrifice, holy and pleasing to God; this is your spiritual worship. Do not be conformed to this age, but be transformed by the renewing of your mind, so that you may discern what is the good, pleasing, and perfect will of God.

Romans 12:1-2

Do everything without grumbling and arguing, so that you may be blameless and pure, children of God who are faultless in a crooked and perverted generation, among whom you shine like stars in the world.

Philippians 2:14-15

Living Forever

So This Is Just the Beginning?

In My Father's house are many dwelling places; if not, I would have told you. I am going away to prepare a place for you. If I go away and prepare a place for you, I will come back and receive you to Myself, so that where I am you may be also.

John 14:2-3

Dear friends, don't let this one thing escape you: with the Lord one day is like 1,000 years, and 1,000 years like one day. The Lord does not delay His promise, as some understand delay, but is patient with you, not wanting any to perish, but all to come to repentance.

2 Peter 3:8-9

For God did not appoint us to wrath, but to obtain salvation through our Lord Jesus Christ, who died for us, so that whether we are awake or asleep, we will live together with Him.

1 Thessalonians 5:9-10

Therefore, brothers, be patient until the Lord's coming. See how the farmer waits for the precious fruit of the earth and is patient with it until he receives the early and the late rains. You also must be patient. Strengthen your hearts, because the Lord's coming is near.

James 5:7-8

This hope does not disappoint.

Romans 5:5

If receiving Christ feels good, wait till you receive all He's got coming to you. *Yes, being a Christian is the greatest thing in the world. And when this world is no more, living with Jesus will only become better than ever.*

So if you have been raised with the Messiah, seek what is above, where the Messiah is, seated at the right hand of God. Set your minds on what is above, not on what is on the earth. . . . When the Messiah, who is your life, is revealed, then you also will be revealed with Him in glory.

Colossians 3:1-2, 4

For the grace of God has appeared, with salvation for all people, instructing us to deny godlessness and worldly lusts and to live in a sensible, righteous, and godly way in the present age, while we wait for the blessed hope and the appearing of the glory of our great God and Savior, Jesus Christ.

Titus 2:11-13

Therefore since we also have such a large cloud of witnesses surrounding us, let us lay aside every weight and the sin that so easily ensnares us, and run with endurance the race that lies before us, keeping our eyes on Jesus, the source and perfecter of our faith, who for the joy that lay before Him endured a cross and despised the shame, and has sat down at the right hand of God's throne.

Hebrews 12:1-2

He will transform the body of our humble condition into the likeness of His glorious body, by the power that enables Him to subject everything to Himself.

Philippians 3:21

Then he showed me the river of living water,
sparkling like crystal, flowing from the throne
of God and of the Lamb down the middle of
the broad street of the city.

On both sides of the river was the tree of
life bearing 12 kinds of fruit, producing its
fruit every month. The leaves of the tree are
for healing the nations, and there will no
longer be any curse.

The throne of God and of the Lamb will
be in the city, and His servants will serve Him.
They will see His face, and His name will be
on their foreheads. Night will no longer exist,
and people will not need lamplight or sunlight,
because the Lord God will give them light.
And they will reign forever and ever.

Revelation 22:1-5

Learn how to live with eternity in your eyes. It changes the look of everything.
One lifetime is just not long enough to experience the wonders of who God is and what He's done. Prepare to be loving Him for this . . . forever.

He has given us a new birth into a living hope through the resurrection of Jesus Christ from the dead, and into an inheritance that is imperishable, uncorrupted, and unfading, kept in heaven for you, who are being protected by God's power through faith for a salvation that is ready to be revealed in the last time.

1 Peter 1:3-5

Therefore we do not give up; even though our outer person is being destroyed, our inner person is being renewed day by day.

2 Corinthians 4:16

I am sure of this, that He who started a good work in you will carry it on to completion until the day of Christ Jesus.

Philippians 1:6

*Look for these other Bible Promise books
to give to the special people in your life.*

**Bible Promises
for Mom**
0-8054-2732-5

**Bible Promises
for Dad**
0-8054-2733-3

**Bible Promises
for My Teacher**
0-8054-2734-1

**Bible Promises
for the Graduate**
0-8054-2741-4

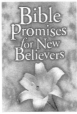

**Bible Promises
for New Believers**
0-8054-2742-2

**Bible Promises
for New Parents**
0-8054-2738-4

**Bible Promises
for Kids**
0-8054-2740-6

**Bible Promises
for Teens**
0-8054-2739-2